CHEERLEADING:
Conditioning for Back Handspring & Tumbling Success!

Rik Feeney

Richardson Publishing
Altamonte Springs, Florida

"Cheerleading: Conditioning for Back Handspring & Tumbling Success!" - Rik Feeney

Richardson Publishing, Inc.
PO Box 162115
Altamonte Springs, FL 32716
www.GymnasticsTrainingTips.com

Copyright © 2007 by Richardson Publishing, Inc.
All Rights Reserved. Printed in the USA.
ISBN: 978-0-9637991-8-0
LOC: 2007921357

DISCLAIMER

This book is written and intended for use as a guide only. The publisher and author are not engaged in the profession of rendering any form of legal, technical, medical, or accounting advice. If for any reason legal, technical, medical, or accounting advice is necessary, you should seek out qualified professionals.

The purpose of this book is to introduce and acquaint individuals with basic safety concepts and strength training methods used in cheerleading, acrobatics, gymnastics, and tumbling. Every effort has been made to provide complete and accurate information on this subject. Readers (athletes) of this book are strongly advised to first get a physical examination by a qualified medical doctor to be cleared for this activity, and then obtain guidance, instruction, and supervision from USAG Safety Certified Coaches or Instructors or Coaches with Risk Management Certifications through the USAG (USA Gymnastics) as well as Certification in First Aid and CPR.

The author and Richardson Publishing shall have neither liability nor responsibility to any person or entity with respect to any injury, loss, or damage caused or alleged to be caused directly or indirectly by the information contained in this book. Any activity, especially one with a high degree of motion, rotation, and height, many times in an inverted (upside-down) position, carries with it a greater potential for injury than normal daily activity. Landing on the head or neck could cause serious and irreparable harm with the potential for fatal consequences to the individual. For this reason, it is advised / demanded that you seek initial training from a Safety Certified gymnastics or cheer coach before using this material for any other purpose.

Warning: Illustrations included with this text are approximations only. Adjustments to equipment, athlete, and training conditions may be required. In addition, all exercises/skills should be spotted by a competent and qualified gymnastics, cheerleading, or tumbling coach until the athlete is competent and confident to do the exercise/skill on her own. Whether an illustration depicts a spotter or not, use one for all athletes training these exercises/drills.

Cheerleading: Conditioning for Back Handspring & Tumbling Success!

What others say...

"As a Physical Therapist and former Certified Athletic Trainer, I feel promoting good mechanics with easy to follow directions provides for less likelihood of poor outcome or injury. I like the easy to apply techniques in this user friendly skill book. The knowledge behind the material encourages success. Great book."

Jennifer Lutzyk, PT

"Great book! I already had some of the cheerleaders read a few of the paragraphs out of the book aloud in class. Maybe they will get the hint, especially about the strength needed to do a back handspring."

Jyl Brown, Elite Gymnastics

"Hi Rik, as a new dance studio owner who teaches basic acrobatics and tumbling your guide provides me and my instructors with much needed information to keep my students safe and conditioned while learning! Thanks so much! "

Kay Terry, Rising Star Family Dance Center / Plaistow, NH

"Great material. I have 2 younger cheer tumbling coaches that I shared it with and they ate it up. I am interested in ordering several copies for reference and pro shop."

Tom Auer, Racine Gymnastics Center / WI

"I thought the information provided in "Conditioning for Back Handspring Success" was great. I have several girls that do privates and I have done some of these exercises with them and I can see a bit of improvement in their back handsprings.

I am currently incorporating these techniques into my intermediate and advanced tumbling class this coming year. I know the kids will definitely benefit.

I think all of the information was presented in a clear, easy to follow format and that I made a wise choice in researching, finding and trying out your products. I am especially excited about the training course for instructors so please keep me informed as to when this one will be available. Keep up the good work."

Shawnte' Washington-Wrice, All Star Tumbling & Cheer / Atoka, OK

"Every tumbler wants to learn a back handspring but doesn't have the strength and flexibility to achieve it. This book will enable you to improve your all around fitness thereby growing strong enough and flexible enough to do them safely! "

Patti Komara / www.pattisallamerican.com / Dyer, IN

CONTENTS

WARNING!

Before starting any program of conditioning it is imperative that the athlete get a physical examination by a qualified medical practitioner to rule out the possibility of heart or other health related risks that could be aggravated or worsened by physical conditioning.

Otherwise healthy looking athletes may have health issues or problems that can be identified by a simple physical examination. Therefore, it is suggested-demanded-commanded that before reading and/or implementing any of the exercises in this book the athlete have a thorough physical examination to rule out any possibility of health risk.

SUPERVISION - Initial Training

While many of the exercises suggested in this text may be performed in a variety of settings (always with proper supervision and adequate safety equipment), the athlete should secure the guidance of a qualified cheer or gym coach to train her in the proper method of performing these exercises.

Each athlete's needs may be different due to different body shape, height, bone length, muscle type, age, physical maturation, previous injury, and needs of the program. For this and possibly other reasons, it is vital to the athlete's health and well-being that a qualified coach adapt the conditioning program as necessary to the needs of the individual athlete.

The coach can perform an initial test to set the base score for the athlete on each exercise and help determine the appropriate exercises (sets, repetitions, resistance, and frequency of training) according to the individual athlete's needs.

Special Note to the Athlete: If you are unwilling to follow the guidelines stated on this page, please donate this book to a library, use it as a doorstop, or if a PDF file; consign it to electronic oblivion. Do not use this book until you complete a physical examination by a doctor and have been cleared medically and have had an evaluation of physical needs (strength & flexibility) by a qualified cheer or gym coach. Sorry, mom's, dad's, and guardians do not count as doctors or coaches.

This book is intended for athletes, coaches, parents, and guardians. Throughout the text, comments will be directed toward coaches and athletes as though you were attending a clinic or workshop. The point of view (who is being talked to at the moment) will shift throughout the document from athlete to coach, so pay close attention.

(Parents should read this text to understand the needs of appropriate and supervised conditioning with the understanding that the coach is responsible and therefore makes the final decision in all training concerns in conjunction with guidance from medical personnel.)

Introduction

Welcome athletes. Hopefully, you have followed the directions on the previous page and had both a physical examination by a medical doctor and a physical evaluation by a qualified coach. If not, DO NOT pass Go, do not collect additional information from this book until you have completed both tasks.[1]

Sorry to be so picky and demanding but safety and proper training are the main goals of this book.

The Big Secret

If ever there was a magical technique for developing impressive tumbling skills; the kind that makes a crowd involuntarily gasp with awe, surprise, and enjoyment – strength would have to be it.

The purpose of this book is to help you increase your base level of strength by 200 to 300%.

---

[1] "Each year, approximately 10 to 13 such cases **[sudden cardiac death]** are reported in the United States. Most young athletes who die unexpectedly from heart disease while participating in sports were not known to have heart disease. Before participating in any sports, young athletes should have a complete physical exam that includes a detailed personal and family history of any heart conditions." *(Preceding notes compiled from American Academy of Pediatrics, Sports Shorts, Sudden Cardiac Death, Issue 9 at http://www.aap.org/family/SportsShorts_09.pdf .)*

Wow! That seems like a huge increase but in reality it is fairly easy for most athletes to achieve. After having a physical evaluation by a coach, you may have found out that you have weaknesses in certain areas. It is fairly common for young ladies to have a weakness in upper body and abdominal strength. As a result, you may not be able to do a single pull-up or leg lift at this time. Again, this is not out of the ordinary; however, you want to become an extraordinary cheerleader so a change must be made.

A 200 to 300% increase in strength starts with the ability to complete one repetition (complete movement of the exercise, for instance, you complete one pull-up).

If your previous evaluation score on pull-ups was 0, and you can now do 1 pull-up, you have increased your strength by 100%. When you can complete two repetitions of the exercise, you will have increased your strength by 200%. And finally, when you can do 4 repetitions of the pull-up you will have increased your strength by 300%. It may not seem so dramatic when presented in this fashion, but you will be pleasantly surprised by how much your tumbling skills improve in relation to your strength development.

The purpose of this book is not to create extensive strength circuits, but to present exercises that can be used to develop a base level of strength, with special emphasis on the core or stabilizing muscles in the torso. The "core stabilizers" enhance both control and power during various tumbling or athletic elements of your routines or skill series.

Once a base level of strength has been appropriately established your coach can develop a shorter, but likely more intense maintenance level conditioning program and switch the focus of training to sport-specific exercises.[2]

Without appropriate strength, the technique used to complete the back handspring will most likely be inadequate and cause you to

---

[2] A sport specific exercise might be a series of back handsprings on the floor. Back handsprings are literally a "multi-joint, patterning exercise" that is specific to the goal of powerful tumbling. You are actually strengthening the muscles used to do a back handspring through repetition of the actual skill.

substitute inferior technical movements that result in poor performance of the skill.

Consistently practicing a technique incorrectly will result in the formation of habitual performance tendencies that will be hard to break once ingrained.

In other words, you practice a bad habit; you get a bad habit.

So, you now know the "big secret" that strength will make you a better and more powerful tumbler. The goal of this book is to help you develop a base level of strength that your coach can build upon with sport specific drills and exercises to not only improve specific skills like back handsprings but to improve overall performance in all drills, skills and routines.

Note: The focus of this book is on strength, however, that does not take away from the very real need to also focus on flexibility, which will be the subject of another book. While working on developing strength, be sure to ask your coach for appropriate warm-up and cool-down stretches beyond the basic stretches listed in this text.

You want it when?

As a former gym club owner and coach, I witnessed an all too common discussion at the front desk when a mother bringing her child into the gym would say to me or the receptionist," *My daughter is trying out for the Cheer Squad at school. She needs a back handspring in two weeks."*

Yikes! Two weeks! (I thought this to myself, then I would ask,) *"Does your daughter have any experience in gymnastics? Can she even do a handstand?"*

In most cases, the answer was *"no"* or the daughter's experience was literally way back when she had a child's body, now she was a young lady entering middle or high school and some of her physical dimensions had changed.

At this point, I am sure the young lady would have ended up in a painful *"nose pose"* if I asked her to do just a simple handstand.[3]

Cheerleading is a sport that requires strength, timing, and cooperation with other members of the squad to perform a great routine. Besides the ability to tumble, having the strength necessary to act as a base and hold other squad members suspended above your head is critically important. And, as a flyer, cheerleaders need enough strength to stay tight and stabilize their bodies so they can be more easily manipulated and safely controlled.

The bottom line is that sufficient strength is a prerequisite for success as a cheerleader whether you tumble or not.

The Basic Goal of this Strength System

The basic goal of this strength system is to increase your overall strength by 200% to 300% using primarily your own body weight as resistance.

This is not a book on bodybuilding or training for Olympic-level fitness, it is an introduction to basic strength techniques that will make the achievement of various sports skills easier to accomplish with an elevated level of technical competence.

The *"no pain, no gain"* philosophy has no place within the structure and guidelines described in this book.

In fact, every athlete embarking on a course of physical development through conditioning is asked to move through this system focusing on form and technique over fatigue and muscle failure.

Athletes that are pushed too hard tend to manipulate body parts into inappropriate positions for the exercise, or engage in some form of *"seizure technique"* in an effort to please the coach and do just one more repetition, or the athlete may "lock-out" joints in an

---

[3] Obviously, this is not always the case, but the prudent coach and/or club owner will always perform a basic evaluation of conditioning and basic tumbling skills before determining placement in the program.

attempt to rest during a set of repetitions, which could produce hyper-extension injury to the joint.

While the goal is to increase strength up to 300%, the achievement of such should take as long as necessary to complete using proper form, technique, and under the supervision of qualified personnel for your safety and that of the other athletes on the squad.

Let's begin with a basic introduction to strength training techniques and concerns in the next chapter.

Strength Training Basics

Several volumes the size of an average encyclopedia set would be required to discuss all aspects of strength training. As such, the following guidelines are presented in a significantly condensed version. The purpose of this guide is to introduce you to basic concepts and then allow you as the athlete (or coach) to research on your own for specific information applicable to your situation.[4]

1.   Supervision

Supervision of the strength training program by qualified coaches and/or medical personnel is important. While many athletes will eventually be able to work this circuit on their own with minimal supervision, at the beginning of the program it is important to have knowledgeable personnel on hand:

- to train the correct techniques for each exercise;

- to make sure the athlete is isolating the proper muscle group[5];

- to make sure appropriate safety conditions are met;

- to determine appropriate match-up of workout partners based on size, strength, and ability;

- to keep athletes "honest" in quantity and quality of exercises performed;

- to plan the strength circuit determining:
  - i.   the exercises performed;
  - ii. the order of performance;
  - iii. traffic flow with other activities taking place;
  - iv. the number of sets;

---

[4] This book is not about weight loss. It is always best to see your doctor about weight loss concerns, body density, eating disorders or self-esteem issues.

[5] To see anatomical illustrations of muscles go to http://www.getbodysmart.com/ap/muscularsystem/menu/menu.html.

    v.   the number of repetitions; and,

   vi. when to increase, decrease, or maintain resistance levels;

- to ensure the safety and layout of equipment being used to perform the strength circuit (i.e., matting, specialty mats, spotting blocks, stall bars, uneven bars, Thera-bands, etc.).

2. Specificity

Strength and/or flexibility are specific to a particular muscle or joint.

Many times the muscles on the "dominant" side of your body are a ¼" to ½" inch bigger than the non-dominant side.

For instance, the leg you push off with into a round off is often slightly larger than your other leg since it is required to do more work during a tumbling workout. In most cases, the difference in strength and size is not noticeable but you should be aware of the possibility. This is one good reason to work not only strength, but as many tumbling skills as are safely possible, on both sides of the body creating what is called bilateral symmetry (a potential equality of strength/flexibility/skill on both sides of the body).

Due to injury, physiological abnormalities, and other factors, the strength and flexibility in one body part may not be the same on one side of the body as the other. For instance, due to a severe sprain on your right ankle the levels of strength and flexibility will be significantly different than your left ankle. Keep this information in mind and adapt strength and/or flexibility exercises with guidance from a sports medicine trained physician in conjunction with your coach.

3. Imbalance causes injury

The muscular system is in many ways dualistic. For every flexor there is an extensor. For instance, to flex the hip joint of your right leg, the quadriceps (the four muscles on top of the thigh) contract lifting the knee of your right leg, while the hamstrings, on the opposite side of the leg act as a brake to slow the knee lift and keep the leg from going beyond its normal range of motion.

When the quadriceps become sufficiently stronger than the hamstrings, or the hamstrings become inflexible through poor training or neglect, a situation is created where the quadriceps can overpower the hamstrings and cause a strain or tear of the hamstrings muscle. This injury is most commonly seen in basketball players making a fast break to run down the court.

Another example would be quick flexion of the upper arm. The biceps cause the arm to flex while the triceps (through eccentric contraction) act as a brake to slow down the motion and prevent injury.

When one muscle group, either the flexor or extensor becomes significantly stronger or less flexible than the opposing muscle group there is a strong potential for injury. Plan your strength circuit accordingly to make sure both the flexor and extensor of a body part receives appropriate attention to prevent potential injury.

4.   Exercise workout order

Start with larger muscle groups in your strength circuit finishing with the smaller muscle groups (or multi-joint exercises to single-joint exercises).

Begin with: *(this is a simplified list)*
- Lower Body:
  - quads
  - hamstrings
  - calf muscles
  - front of lower leg
  - inner thigh
  - outer thigh
- Abdominals & Back:
  - stomach (upper, middle, lower)
  - hip flexors
  - back muscles
- Upper Body:
  - chest
  - shoulders
  - arms

5. Resistance

In almost all exercises represented in this book, the only resistance used will be some portion of the athlete's body weight. Shifting the athlete's body position to require the muscles being exercised to produce more effort will be the method most often employed to increase resistance.

No weights or machines will be used, except possibly surgical tubing, or Thera-bands[6] to provide some resistance. Equipment such as matting, or chin-up bars will be used to work around or on, or even used to stabilize body parts, however, the resistance will still be the athlete's own weight. The amount of resistance used will be determined based on how effectively that athlete can perform the exercise using proper form and technique.

Increasing Resistance

An example of increasing resistance might be starting your bent knee push-ups on an incline mat. Place your hands at the high end of the incline mat and your knees on the floor exercise carpet at the low end of the mat. Once you are able to effectively complete your sets at this level, you would increase resistance by moving your hands down the incline mat until (eventually) both hands and knees are on the floor. The next increase would be to straighten your legs. To continue increasing resistance as you grow stronger, you might put your feet up on one panel mat. To increase your range of motion on this exercise, place two panel mats in an ever widening "V" formation on the floor. Put both of your feet on the mats where they come together at the bottom of the "V" and both of your hands on the respective mats where they widen, so you can lower your chest down between the mats on each push-up working a wider range of motion.

Note: There will come a point when raising your legs by adding more mats changes the exercise from primarily a chest (pectorals) and arms exercise to a shoulder (anterior deltoid) and arms exercise. Consult with your coach to make sure you are still giving proper attention to all body parts as you reconfigure your strength circuits.

---

[6] http://www.thera-band.com/

6.   Repetitions

A repetition is a single performance of an exercise, such as one pull-up.

In general, the athlete will work 8 to 12 repetitions of an exercise (one set) before increasing the resistance by shifting body angle to create increased resistance.

Repetitions vs. Time

Sometimes your coach may recommend minimum repetitions of an exercise, such as 10 push-ups as your goal. Sometimes the coach may prescribe a time frame such as 15 to 30 seconds for you to complete as many of the exercises with form and technique as you can within the allotted time frame, whether it be 10, 15, or 20 repetitions. The key is form and technique. It also allows other squad members that are stronger to work within their capabilities and those that are weaker to work to the best of their current abilities.

7.   Sets

One "set" is comprised of the prescribed number of repetitions of an exercise you must complete. For instance, the coach may request that you do two sets of 10 push-ups. You do 10 push-ups, rest for 30 seconds, and then do 10 more push-ups to complete the second set.

In the beginning of the season, and for strength training purposes, the coach may prescribe 8 to 12 different exercises with one or two sets of repetitions as part of a strength circuit. Once the basic strength goal has been achieved by all athletes, the coach may then develop a shorter but still intense strength circuit to maintain the base level of strength but will often focus on more "sport-specific" training during workouts. Sport-specific training simply means using the actual skills being performed such as back handsprings or split leaps as the basis of developing appropriate levels of strength, timing, and sequence of movement patterns.

8. Frequency of Circuits

Most fitness enthusiasts have the tendency to jump into the deep end of training and immerse themselves in several workouts a week without providing proper intervals of rest and recuperation. Enthusiasm must be applauded, but common sense and patience should prevail by starting with 2 workouts a week for one month, then progressing to 3 times a week (based on appropriate progress) for the following month.

Apologies to all involved for the next statement, but *"a lack of planning is not justification for an extreme conditioning program at the eleventh hour."* A last minute, intense workout program presents a strong potential for injury.

48 Hours

Some coaches may opt to train upper body exercises M-W-F, and lower body exercises T-Th-S, however, it may be best to start with a whole body circuit that incorporates a 48-hour rest period in between. So, if you do a strength circuit Monday at 7:00pm, your next strength workout would be Wednesday at 7:00pm or 48 hours later to allow for rest and recuperation.

Vacation Time

Another good idea is to create an interval training system where every six to eight weeks you take a week off from conditioning or at the very least cut the intensity of the strength workouts by 50%.

Maintenance

Once you reach a specific strength goal, your coach may design a strength circuit that is shorter but possibly more intense to cover all the major muscle groups to keep them in appropriate condition while adding more "sport-specific" exercises to the workout like multiple passes of back handsprings which are now not only skills but conditioning to build strength in the specific muscles used in the appropriate sequence and timing.

9.   Breathing

Based on some research of web sites, there may be some controversy over correct breathing technique. In this text, the suggestion for breathing during exercise will follow the guideline suggested at the Georgetown University Hospital site, "Exhale as you begin the movement."[7] It seems to make sense, if you want the full range of motion on a sit up; you need to breathe out as you begin the movement.

> **Warning:** Do not hold your breath while straining to complete a repetition of an exercise or while holding an isometric (non-moving) exercise. It is possible to burst capillaries in your face, eyes, and ears by holding your breath while applying excessive strain or force to complete the exercise, which could lead to severe injury.

10. Positive & Negative Movement

There are two types of movement in any exercise described as positive and negative movements. A **positive** movement is normally considered the action that actually causes movement and causes the muscle tissue to contract. A **negative** movement occurs when you return to the start position of the exercise usually through eccentric contraction or the controlled lengthening of muscle tissue.

For example, on a pull-up the positive motion would occur when you bend your arms and lift your chin above the bar. The negative motion would occur when you lower in a controlled fashion back to the long hang position ready to start another repetition.

Timing

The key to any effective exercise is that it is safely performed. Toward that end you may want to consider using a timing sequence of 1 second for the positive movement and 3 seconds

---

[7] Proper breathing during exercise.
http://www.georgetownuniversityhospital.org/body.cfm?id=555563&action=articleDetail&AEProductID=Adam2004_10&AEArticleID=000388 Review Date: 10/3/2005. Reviewed By: A.D.A.M. Medical Illustration Team.

for the negative movement. For example, on the pull-up, take one second to pull-up, and then take three seconds to lower in a controlled fashion back to the start position.

This method may also help to reduce muscle soreness the day after a strength circuit by cutting down on the micro-tears that may occur in muscle tissue due to the effects of the myotic reflex. The "myotic" or stretch reflex is a safety mechanism designed to keep a muscle from going beyond its normal range of motion by quickly attempting to contract the muscle.

For instance, if you drop out of a pull-up too quickly, the myotic reflex may kick in to keep you from going beyond a normal range of motion; however, the force of the drop may cause the contracting muscle tissue to develop micro-tears as the force of the fall overpowers the contraction, resulting in sore muscles the next day.

Negatives can be Positive

As stated above, a negative motion occurs when you return, in a controlled fashion, to the start position for another repetition of an exercise. A negative or **eccentric motion** occurs when a force or resistance causes a shortened or contracted muscle to extend, possibly while still attempting to contract. Slowly lowering from a pull-up is one example of eccentric motion.

When you were first evaluated, you may have been unable to do even one pull-up. At this point your body weight is too much resistance. You can adapt the pull-up exercise by getting an assist from a spotter or by putting one foot on a lower bar and using it to assist in the pull-up, or you can start by doing negatives of the exercise. (See "Negative Pull-ups" on page 32.)

Negative Exercise

A negative exercise simply means you start at the fully contracted position of the muscle being focused on, and then slowly lower (about 3 to 4 seconds) to the normal start position of the exercise.

For instance starting with a low bar, or by putting a spotting block next to a raised bar, you can reach out to the bar and start at the top of a pull-up by stepping off the block and briefly holding your chin above the bar, and then slowly lower your body by extending your arms to the count of thousand one..., thousand two..., thousand three..., thousand four..., until you are in a long hang position under the bar. Repeat the procedure for the full set of repetitions by putting your feet back on the block and climbing back into the "chin above the bar position."

In future sets of pull-ups (or whatever exercise) see how many pull-ups you can do positively first, even if it is only one, before switching to the negative aspect of the exercise.

Consult your Coach

Like the first day of school, you have been introduced to a variety of subjects – only these revolve around the concept of conditioning. This brief introduction cannot hope to cover every area of concern regarding the development of an appropriate strength circuit specific to your needs; only your coach or a doctor with a sports medicine background can do that. Remember to get a physical examination by your doctor, a physical evaluation by your coach, and keep records of your progress to track when changes need to be made.

Suggested Exercises

On the following pages you'll find a series of "suggested" exercises grouped generally by body part. The term "suggested" is specifically chosen because the need for any of the exercises listed should be determined after an evaluation by a qualified cheer or gymnastics coach.

When developing a circuit of exercises for an individual or a group, determine the dominant need first, next, move on to peripheral exercises that are helpful but not critical.

When applying reality as the common denominator, it will soon become apparent due to time constraints, availability of equipment, frequency of workouts, and other factors that developing a strength circuit with no more than 12 to 14 exercises is best.

As stated in a previous section, start your circuit with larger muscle groups first, working progressively toward smaller muscles or muscle groups. When developing the strength circuit, make sure both sides of a muscle group (flexor / extensor) are represented.

Illustrations

While each of the illustrations presented in this book is intended to demonstrate the performance of each exercise, it should be kept in mind that due to photographic constraints and limited space, illustrations included with this text are approximations only. Adjustments to equipment, athlete, and training conditions may be required. In addition, all skills should be supervised and/or spotted by a competent and qualified cheerleading or tumbling coach until the athlete is competent and confident to do the exercise on her own. Whether an illustration depicts supervision or the use of a spotter or not, use one for all athletes training these drills.

Additional resources:

My talents at illustration are limited to a camera and software, so accurate depictions of the muscles being worked in a particular exercise are beyond my ability, however, you can go online and Google "human anatomy" and/or "muscular system."

One such site for muscular descriptions/illustrations is
http://www.getbodysmart.com/ap/muscularsystem/menu/menu.html

Another site for additional information on exercise is
http://adam.about.com/reports/000029_1.htm

Exercises for the Legs

In this section, the focus is on leg exercises. Most of the time, your athletes will have adequate leg strength, however, cheerleading is not like most activities in that it contains explosive leaps, jumps, and controlled landings. Focusing on proper leg conditioning will provide the athlete with the appropriate power to focus on technique and form, not just "going through the motions" of the skill.

Exercise: Tuck Jumps on Landing Cushion

Purpose: This exercise will help develop the quadriceps, the four muscles of the upper leg above the knee.

Set up: Place an 8-inch landing cushion on top of the floor exercise mat. One or two athletes may perform this exercise at one time; however, more than two could create the potential for collision during the several repetitions of the skill.

Directions: The athlete stands well within the boundaries of the mat in a stretch position. The athlete performs a tuck jump bringing her knees up to her chest and then quickly extending her legs to a landing on the cushion with her knees slightly bent to absorb the force of landing. The athlete immediately performs the next and subsequent tuck jumps for the remainder of the timed exercise.

Duration: 15 seconds during the initial training of the exercise. The exercise may increase in 15 second increments over the next four weeks (30, 45, 60). Increases in time for each set should only occur when the athlete is capable of performing the tuck jumps consistently and without pause at the lower time increments.

Safety Notes: Train the athlete to land with her knees slightly apart to keep them from banging together on landing, and with both feet facing forward to help prevent rolling of the ankle on landing. It is important for the athlete to maintain awareness of her position during the exercise to keep from landing with one foot on the mat and one foot off, or with an ankle on the edge of the mat, which could lead to a sprain, and to keep from encroaching on another athlete's training area which could lead to a collision.

Exercise: Reverse Leg Lift – Floor

Purpose: To build the hamstring muscle group on the upper thigh on the back of the leg. The hamstrings are responsible for quick extension of the hip angle, whereas the quads and associated muscles are responsible for flexion or closing of the hip angle as demonstrated in the peak of the tuck jump above.

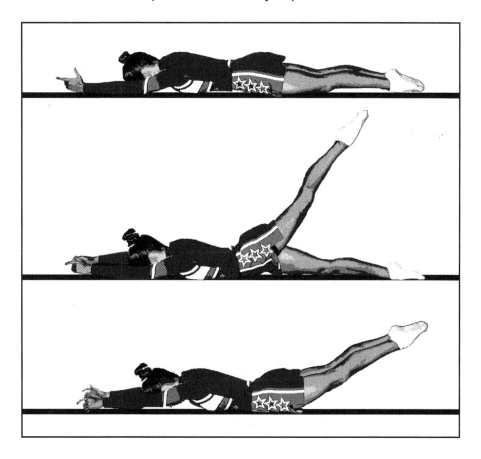

Set up: The only thing needed for this exercise is a comfortable mat or the floor exercise carpet.

Directions: The athlete is in a prone (lying face downward) position on the mat with both arms above her head and next to her ears. The objective is to lift one leg at a time as high as possible, without rolling the hips laterally, and hold at the peak of the lift for 5 seconds. To stabilize her upper body, the athlete may hold a low stall bar or the base of some piece of equipment (preferably not in use at the time).

The exercise may also be done lifting both legs at the same time and holding at the peak for 5 seconds. To increase the range of motion of the legs, the athlete can start the exercise on a folded panel mat.

Duration: Have the athlete work sets of 8 to 15 repetitions.

Exercise: Reverse Leg Lift – Incline Mat

This exercise is done exactly the same as "Exercise: Reverse Leg Lift – Floor" with the exception that the athlete is in a prone position on an incline mat with her head at the high end of the mat and her feet at the low end of the mat.

Exercise: Reverse Leg Lift – Stall Bars

Purpose: Same as Reverse Leg Lift – Floor.

Set Up: Place an incline mat against a set of stall bars so the wide end of the mat is on the floor and the narrow end is at the top.

Directions: The athlete hangs from the top bar of the stall bars facing toward the wall so the front of her body is in contact with the incline mat. From this position, the objective is to lift one leg at a time as high as possible, without rolling the hips laterally, and hold at the peak of the lift for 5 seconds.

The exercise may also be done lifting both legs at the same time and holding at the peak for 5 seconds.

Duration: Have the athlete work sets of 8 to 15 repetitions.

Exercise: Seated Leg Extensions – Lat Pulls / Floor
(with Frisbee / Carpet Square)

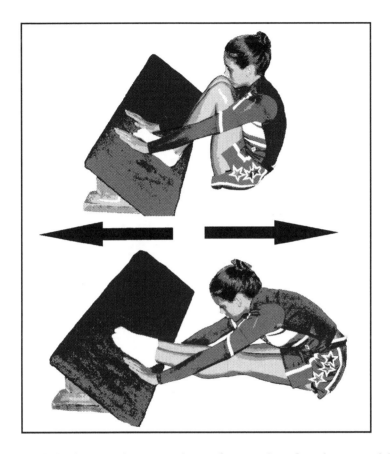

Purpose: This is another version of exercise for the quadriceps, which also works a portion of the arms (triceps and latissimus dorsai) on the return to start motion.

Set up: A section of the floor exercise carpet next to a wall and a carpet square or Frisbee.

Directions: The athlete places a Frisbee upside-down on the floor exercise carpet in front of a wall. The athlete actually sits in the Frisbee, or on top of a carpet square (remnant) in a tuck position so she can place her feet and hands on the wall. The objective is for the athlete to push her legs away from the wall until her legs are fully extended.

The "Lat Pull" portion of the exercise begins when the athlete uses her arms to return to the tuck position against the wall by placing her hands on the carpet next to her knees; she presses down on the floor to lift her hips slightly so she can slide back to the start position.

Duration: 8 to 15 repetitions.

Exercise: Side Lunges

Purpose: To help build the muscles of the inner thigh called the adductors, the primary muscles used in bringing the legs together.

Set Up: A tumbling strip can be used or one side of the floor exercise carpet.

Directions: Traveling sideways, the athlete takes a step to her left into a side lunge position, and then pulls her right leg to close with her left back in a standing position. She repeats this sideways lunge walk down the length of the floor exercise carpet. She should return to her starting position facing the same direction but leading into each lunge with the opposite (or right) leg back down the floor exercise carpet.

Duration: Start with 4 to 6 passes on each leg and slowly progress in subsequent workouts up to 8 to 10 passes on each leg.

Exercise: Side Leg Lifts

Purpose: "Side Lunges" work primarily the adductors or the muscles on the inner thigh that are used to bring your legs together. And, while the abductors, muscles that lift your legs away from each other, are used in each step of those exercises, not as much resistance is placed on them as in "Side Leg Lifts."

Set Up: A tumbling strip can be used or one side of the floor exercise carpet.

Directions: The athlete starts by lying on her side on the floor. She can bend her bottom leg for better control or balance if she wishes. The objective is for the athlete to lift her leg up and away from her body to the highest point she can reach without turning out her hips or reaching a point where the resistance is diminished. She then lowers her leg slowly back to the start position. After each set switch legs and repeat.

Duration: Start with 2 sets of 10 lifts on each leg before increasing resistance.

Note: You can increase resistance for this exercise by having the athlete move to a wedge mat with her feet at the low end, adding small ankle weights, doing it from a stand next to a beam, or adding a Thera-band of various resistance levels.

Exercise: Heel Raises

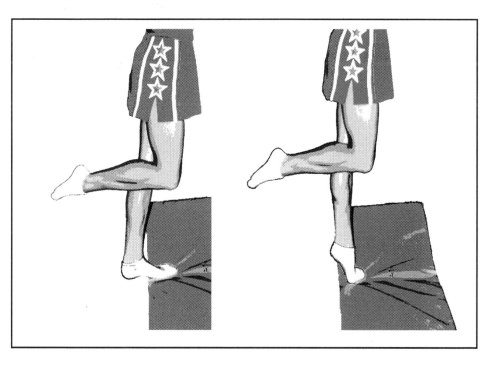

Purpose: This exercise is good for strengthening the gastrocnemius and soleus, collectively and more commonly called the calf muscles, located on the back of the lower leg.

Set Up: Take a folded panel mat and place it in on the floor exercise carpet right next to the wall.

Directions: The athlete steps onto the panel mat so the balls of her feet are on the edge of the mat with her heels extended over the edge. She then lifts her right leg until the calf of her right leg is just touching the inside of her left knee. From this position, the athlete presses down through the ball of her left foot until her heel is as high as possible and she is in a position called "high toe." Alternate your feet after each set of repetitions.

Duration: Start with 30 seconds worth of repetitions on each leg for two sets on each leg. Increase to 45, then 60 seconds as strength improves.

Safety: The timing of this exercise should be one second to raise her heel and three seconds to lower her heel, preferably below the level of the mat to work through the widest range of motion possible. Cue the athlete to pay attention to her foot position and balance so she does not slip off the mat during the exercise.

Exercises for Arms & Shoulder Girdle

Exercise: Bent Knee Push-ups

Purpose: The main focus on this exercise is to improve strength across the athlete's chest muscle or pectoralis major.

Set Up: This exercise can be performed on a panel mat or the floor exercise carpet.

Directions: From her knees to her head the athlete strives to keep a tight and straight body position with her hands placed on the floor directly below her shoulders. Her hands should be turned in slightly and shoulder-width apart. The athlete performs a repetition of the skill by bending her arms and lowering until she can just touch her chin to the floor – no other part of her body, other than hands, knees, and chin should come in contact with the floor.

Duration: Start with 2 sets of 15 seconds worth of repetitions. The idea is to keep moving and not allow the athlete to rest on her stomach at any time during the set. You can increase the time to 30, 45, and 60 seconds based on the athlete's performance in subsequent weeks.

Safety: Focus on form. Many athletes as they tire will attempt to rest on the floor, or turn their hands out and lock their elbows at the peak of the push-up, which could lead to potential injury. If this is the case, do not increase the duration of the set until the athlete can perform each repetition with correct form.

Exercise: Push-ups

The directions and safety comments are the same as for the "Bent Knee Push-ups" with the obvious and notable exception that the athlete keeps her legs straight during the performance of this exercise.

Safety: Weaker athletes may allow their stomachs to sag causing a rocking forward and subsequent rocking backward during the push-up phase which could put undue pressure on the lower back. If this occurs, have the athlete return to "Bent Knee Push-ups" until she has enough abdominal strength to maintain the hollow position on each repetition.

Exercise: R.O.M. Push-ups

R.O.M. stands for "range of motion," which in the case of exercises means the widest range of motion safely possible.

Push-ups over a flat surface do not actually put the pectorals through a full range of motion. Once the athlete has demonstrated proficiency with a regular push-up, she can place two panel mats in front of her that are her shoulder-width apart. By placing one hand on each mat while keep both feet down on the floor exercise carpet, the athlete lowers into the push-ups allowing her chest to go below her hands, or in between the mats, until she feels a stretch in her chest muscles, and then pushes back up to a brief support position before lowering into the next repetition of the exercise.

Safety: Begin with the feet lower than the athlete's body as you expand the range of motion on this exercise. There will be less weight on her hands initially, which you can change simply by raising her higher each week as she demonstrates proficiency and appropriate strength development.

Note: Another method for changing not only range of motion, but exercising different aspects of the same muscle is to change hand placement. For instance placing the hands together in an almost a triangular position (see illustration below).

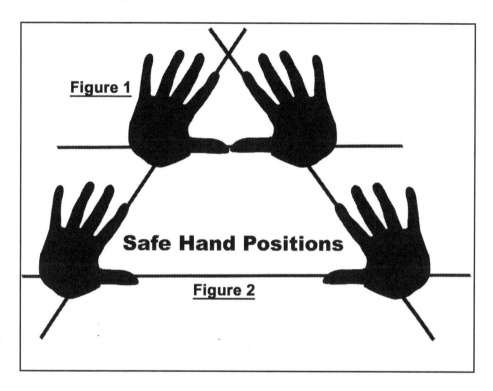

Figure 1

Safe Hand Positions

Figure 2

Figure 2 depicts the normal hand placement on a push-ups exercise, while **Figure 1** demonstrates a different hand position to work a different aspect or portion of the muscle group in question.

Safety Note: At no time should the athlete be allowed to turn her hands out (fingers of respective hands pointing east and west) and lock or hyperextend her elbows. Many times the athlete does this to rest in the middle of a set. The focus should be on form and safety. Warn the athlete of the potential for injury because of incorrect hand placement. If the athlete is still incapable of completing the repetitions of a set without resorting to this tactic, lower the number of repetitions in each set until she can perform them safely and with proper form.

Exercise: Triceps Push-ups

Purpose: The main goal of this exercise is to help strengthen the triceps, the muscles on the back of the upper arm; however, this exercise is also helpful for strengthening the anterior deltoid, the muscle on the front of the shoulders, which helps when punching out of the floor on front handsprings and back handsprings.

Set Up: This exercise can be practiced off the edge of a tumble tramp or with a stack of folded panel mats or spotting block placed against a wall.

Directions: The athlete stands her back to the spotting block, or may even start by sitting on the edge of the block and placing both hands at her sides. She lifts her hips off the block by pressing down on the block with her arms, then shifts her hips a few inches forward, and lowers by bending her arms until she can feel a stretch in her shoulder muscles. The athlete presses from this lowered position until her arms are straight before lowering into the next repetition of the exercise.

Duration: Start with 2 sets of 15 seconds each and increase in 15-second increments in subsequent weeks as proficiency and strength increase.

Safety: Make sure the object being used (tumble tramp, mats, or block) is stable and securely fastened in place, to prevent injuries to the athlete's shoulders and potentially outstretched arms should the object slip or move mid-exercise. Cue the athlete to focus on her hand position throughout to make sure she does not slip off her support during the set of repetitions.

Exercise: Carpet Cleaners

Purpose: This exercises focuses on developing strength in the anterior deltoid (front of shoulder muscle). Development of this muscle is one of the keys to real power tumbling.

Set Up: This exercise is performed on the floor exercise carpet.

Directions: The athlete starts in a seated pike position with both hands at her sides with fingertips pointing toward her toes. The athlete presses down through her arms lifting her hips slightly off the floor. With her hips slightly off the floor the athlete pushes her hips backward until her hands finish lined up with her ankles (depending on her hamstring flexibility).

Duration: Start with two passes (pass = length of the floor exercise carpet, usually 42 feet) and increase by two passes each week as proficiency and strength increase until the athlete can complete 8 to 10 passes.

Safety: To keep the athlete from sustaining carpet burns on the back of her legs, it is a good idea to have her wear gym shorts and socks while performing this exercise. Another option may be to have the athlete sit on a carpet square or place one under her feet to prevent rug burns to her heels.

Exercise: Wrist Push-ups

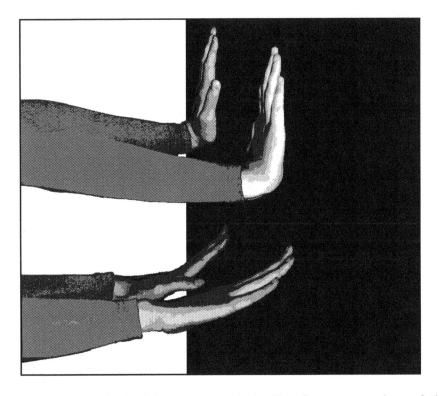

Purpose: To help build up strength in the flexor muscles of the forearm crossing the wrist joint.

Set Up: The athlete will need a wall free of obstruction for this exercise.

Directions: The athlete stands in front of a wall so that with her arms stretched in front of her, her fingertips can just barely touch the wall. From this position, the athlete leans forward placing her hands flat against the wall with her hands turned toward each other in a slightly triangular position. The objective is for the athlete to press down through her hands until she can press off the wall almost to her fingertips. **Note:** At the outset, the athlete may only be able to press up until the palm of her hand is free from the wall.

Duration: Start with two sets of 15 seconds for the first week, then increase in increments of 15 seconds to 30, 45, and 60 seconds in subsequent weeks as proficiency and strength increase. **Note:** To add resistance simply increase the angle of the athlete's body until she can ultimately perform this exercise with her body at a 45 degree angle.

Exercise: Roll-Up Drill

Purpose: This is a good exercise for working the extensor muscles that cross the wrist on the upper part of the forearm.

Set Up: Obtain a wooden dowel, (a cylindrical piece of wood) about 18-inches long and 1-inch in diameter, then attach to the middle of the dowel a piece of rope 24-36 inches long of sufficient strength to easily hold a five-pound weight.

Directions: The athlete will hold the dowel on either side of the rope with her arms straight out in front of her and attempt to rewind the rope around the dowel – lifting the 5 pound weight upward closer to the dowel.

Safety: Do not drop the weight on your toes – it hurts like the dickens, and you may let slip your advanced knowledge of colorful vocabulary.

Exercise: Negative Pull-ups

Purpose: To help develop the strength to perform a normal pull-up, which builds strength in the triceps and latissimus dorsi muscles.

Set Up: This skill can be performed on a chin-up bar, high bar, or the upper rail of the uneven bars. **Note:** The bar does not need to be any higher than the length of the athlete's body plus her arms, so that when hanging from the bar her toes could just brush the floor.

Place a stable spotting block or stack of mats off to one side of the bar.

Note: A "negative" exercise is when the athlete starts in the finish position (muscle contracted) and slowly through eccentric motion (lengthening of the muscle or relaxing of the contraction) returns to the "start" position. A negative is used when an athlete does not possess sufficient strength to complete one full repetition of the exercise without some form of assistance.

Directions: From a stand on the spotting block (figure 1) the athlete grabs the bar (hands shoulder-width apart) and jumps up slightly to hang by her hands so that her eyes are level with the bar (figure 2). After momentarily holding this position, the athlete slowly lowers (2-3 seconds) to a hanging position (figures 3 & 4). By placing one foot on the spotting block she can step back up and start the next repetition of this exercise.

Duration: Start with 4 to 6 repetitions of this skill, increasing to 8 to 10, then 10 to 12 repetitions.

Ideally, once the athlete is able to complete one normal pull-up, the logical progression from this exercise, she should do so without aid of the block. She can then continue with negatives for the rest of the set.

Exercise: Low Bar Pull-Ups with Block

Purpose: To enable the athlete to perform the positive action of the pull-up with an assist from her legs.

Set Up: Place a small spotting block or two folded and stacked panel mats two to three feet in front of a low bar rail.

Directions: The athlete grabs hold of the low bar in an overgrip with her hands set shoulder-width apart, and then places her feet, one at a time, on the spotting block / stacked mats so that she is hanging from the bar with her body in a piked position. The athlete begins the pull-up using her feet just enough to help her make the pull-up above the bar. She then lowers slowly to the start position and begins the next repetition until the set is finished.

Duration: Start with 4 to 6 repetitions and increase incrementally as proficiency and strength increase or until the athlete can progress to normal pull-ups on the high bar.

Exercise: Tiptoe Pull-Ups

This is the next logical progression from "Low Bar Pull-ups with a Block." The athlete hangs from the high bar of a set of uneven bars facing toward the low bar. Similar to the above drill, the athlete will lift one leg so her toe touches the low bar and she can push off the bar just enough to do a pull-up or to help her complete a set of pull-ups.

Exercise: Pull-Ups

Finally! The athlete starts in a long hang position with an overgrip that is shoulder width apart and smoothly pulls her head above the bar and then lowers carefully to the start position to begin her next repetition.

Note: This exercise may be combined with "Tip Toe Pull-ups" until the athlete has developed sufficient strength to make it through a complete set without assistance.

Safety: To prevent injury, unplanned dismounts, and disruption to workout partners "seizure technique" is not allowed. The body should remain straight and stretched throughout the pull-up; the only motion being the bending of the arms. Any other jerking, bouncing at the bottom, kicking the legs, or withdrawal into a fetal position is not an acceptable technique for the performance of this exercise.

Exercise: Chin-ups

Purpose: To build strength in the biceps muscle on the front of the upper arm, which is used to flex or bend the arm.

Note: Pull-ups are overgrip with hands shoulder-width apart working more of the latissimus dorsai and triceps; chin-ups are undergrip with hands 6 to 8 inches apart and focus primarily on the biceps as the primary mover of this exercise.

Directions: This exercise may be initiated similar to the "pull-up from a block," on a low bar, or using toes. The only difference in performance is the grip style and width of hand placement. Chin-ups may also be performed with a closer undergrip in a fashion like the "Under Bar Rowing" exercise.

<u>**Special Safety Note:**</u> **For all chin-up, pull-up, and lat pull-up style exercises, it may be safest to start the athlete on a bar low enough that she can put her feet on the floor in case she loses her grip on the bar.**

It is quite common for the muscles in the forearm and hand to tire faster than the muscles of the upper arm and shoulder. As a result, the athlete's forearm begins to numb and she may complain of not being able to maintain her grip as the smaller muscles tire and lose their ability to function, which could cause the athlete to lose her grip and fall from the bar at an inopportune moment.

Abdominal Exercises

While strength in the legs and the arms is certainly an important prerequisite to performing dynamic back handsprings and other tumbling skills, it is the mid-section of the body, both abdominals and lower back muscles that may have the most dramatic effect on the technical aspects of tumbling skills.

Basic Biomechanics

In short, force travels in a straight line. If the muscles of the torso do not act as "core stabilizers" (i.e., the abdominals and lower back muscles primarily) to maintain alignment, then the athlete's body will not be able to maintain a straight or slightly hollowed line. The force or power of the skill will be diminished as power is siphoned off in directions of no benefit to the performance of the skill.

As an example, imagine an athlete is standing in front of you with both arms straight out in front of her – and a port-a-pit in back of her for safety.

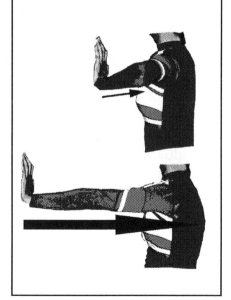

If you grabbed hold of her wrists and pushed forward and the athlete allowed her arms to bend; where would the force of the motion go? Basically, the force went in a straight line down her forearm and out her elbows into space with very little force being transferred to her torso. And, if you don't believe the force went out her elbows, try sticking your face in back of her elbow while somebody else pushes through her arms in a similar fashion.

Actually, please don't do that, or you will end up literally with your nose out of joint. I was exaggerating to make a point that the force continues out through her elbow, but there is nothing there for it to act on.

Let's try this again, except this time the athlete keeps her arms tight while you grab her wrists and push forward. This time, since the force is going straight through her arms, it gets transferred through her shoulders to her body and she will most likely fall backward, which, by the way, is why you put a port-a-pit in back of her before starting this demonstration.

Now, think of what happens when an athlete does a back handspring and lands in the handstand position with her hips piked – too scary to contemplate right? What if she lands with a loose arch? She won't crash near as bad as the piked position but she will most likely fall back in the direction from which she started the skill.

"Core stability" the main reason for this section, and probably the key to effective tumbling begins with the exercises listed here.

The legs may propel the athlete into the skill, and the arms may support, punch, or lift the athlete, but the core stabilizers control the direction force will travel through the athlete's body and ultimately determine the level of technique in most tumbling skills.

Unfortunately, many athletes have very poor abdominal strength and should be taught an incremental method of building strength in this area. The easiest test for strength in this area is to ask the athlete to do a forward roll to a stand. A forward roll, done correctly, does not make use of the arms pushing off the floor after tucking the head over and rolling, instead the athlete should reach straight up to finish in a stand in stretch position. If the athlete is incapable of doing this without putting her hands down, putting a knee down, twisting to the side or any other form of seizure technique – she needs to develop her abdominal muscles in a gradual and progressive manner.

Exercise: Rock'n Roll on Panel Mat

Purpose: To use a bit of motion to assist in the proper performance of this abdominal exercise.

Set Up: Two stacked and folded panel mats placed on the floor exercise carpet.

Directions: Have the athlete sit down on the end of the stacked panel mats with both arms up next to her ears. The objective is to have the athlete rock backwards carefully until her hands contact the mat and her knees are tucked to her chest, and then roll forward until her feet touch the floor and continue through to a standing stretch position.

Duration: Start with 15 second sets allowing the athlete to complete as many as safely possible (this is not a speed contest) for 2 or 3 sets. Each week add 15 seconds to 30, 45, and 60-second sets.

Safety: The athlete sits down on the mat keeping her upper body straight up and down and rocking backwards – do not allow her to throw her head and shoulders backward as this could cause severe injury. The idea is to stop the rocking motion as the hands take on weight to keep the athlete from compressing her neck or straining tendons in her neck. In addition, cue the athlete to hold her knees slightly apart during this exercise to keep her from accidentally bopping herself in the face.

Exercise: Upper Crunches

Purpose: To work on the upper range of the rectus abdominus muscle.

Set Up: This exercise can be performed on the floor exercise carpet or a panel mat.

Directions: From a layout position the athlete places both hands behind her ears so her fingertips just touch her head. Next, she bends both knees so her heels are just touching her rear end. The athlete then allows her knees to lower to the mat on either side so the bottoms of her feet are touching. From this position, the athlete will roll her head and shoulders upward and slightly forward until her shoulder blades just come off the mat. She will hold this position for a three-second count and then carefully lower back to the floor or mat and repeat according to the repetitions prescribed for each set.

Duration: Start with sets of 5-10 crunches and each week attempt to add 5 additional crunches until the athlete can complete 30 crunches in one set.

Safety: Never, ever allow the athlete to lock her fingers together in back of her head. When tired or not concentrating the athlete may pull too hard and strain neck muscles or compress the neck which could cause an injury.

Exercise: Lower Crunches

Purpose: To help develop the lower range of motion of the rectus abdominus.

Set Up: Same as Upper Crunches exercise.

Directions: From a layout position, the athlete places both hands palms down at her sides on the floor. She then bends her knees until they are a few inches from her chest with her heels resting on the backs of her thighs. From this position, the athlete uses her lower abdominal muscles to roll her hips up and off the ground until just her lower back is in contact with the floor. This position is held for 3 seconds and then the athlete carefully rolls her hips back down to the floor.

Duration: Same as Upper Crunches.

Exercise: ½ Sit Up

Purpose: To focus on and strengthen the mid-range of the rectus abdominus muscle.

Set Up: This exercise can be performed on the floor with a partner to hold the athlete's feet, or she can place her feet carefully under a larger mat or piece of equipment. (Make sure either the mat or equipment is stable and will not fall on or trap the athlete's feet.)

Directions: Sitting in a tuck position, with feet securely held in place, the athlete lowers her body backward about half the distance from the upright position to the floor, and then returns to the start position.

Arm Placement: Arm placement can make a difference in the amount of resistance during this exercise. To start, the athlete can cross her arms across her chest, touching her elbows to her knees and then immediately lowering into the next half sit up. The idea is not to come to a full sitting position which would take the tension off the abdominal muscles and allow the athlete, in effect, to rest.

To add resistance, the athlete can raise her arms higher by lifting her elbows up and out and touching her fingertips to her head just in back of her ears. For even more resistance, she can raise her arms straight above her head throughout the exercise.

Exercise: Tuck Sit ups

Purpose: To build strength in the abdominal muscles and hip flexors.

Set Up: Same as Crunches

Directions: From a layout position on the floor, the athlete pulls through her abdominal and hip flexor muscles to sit up into a tuck position. While the illustration does not depict this, the athlete should NOT lower completely to the floor on each exercise but should lower to a "rocker drill" position with her feet approximately six-inches above the floor, and her upper body lowering until she can just touch the bottom of her shoulder blades on the floor. Again, the idea is to maintain tension on the affected muscles throughout the entire set and not allow a rest after each repetition.

Note: Stopping before a resting position on the floor also helps to eliminate the potential for lower back injury as the athlete arches her back and then snaps it down to the floor in an attempt to help "kip" her up into the next sit up. (*Us old dogs may be ugly and out of shape, but we know all the tricky ways to, shall we say, "innocently but inappropriately" perform the exercise.*)

Exercise: Incline Mat Leg Lift

Purpose: To work full range of motion exercises with the abdominals and hip flexors allowing gravity to add some additional resistance.

Set Up: Place an incline or wedge mat on the floor exercise carpet or an open panel mat.

Directions: The athlete starts in layout position with her head at the high end of the incline mat and both arms up next to her ears. You may also place the incline mat in front of some stall bars so the athlete can grab hold of a lower bar or she can grab hold of the top of the incline mat to stabilize her body position.

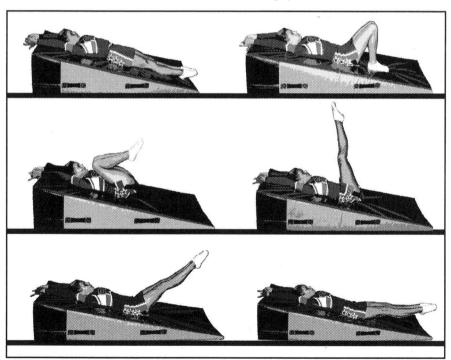

The athlete then tucks her knees up to her chest and continues rolling upward until her hips are off the incline mat. She then extends her legs until they are straight and lowers them down to a hollow position with her heels a few inches off the mat before starting the next repetition. Do not allow her to lower all the way to the mat and rest between repetitions.

Duration: 5 to 10 leg lifts, adding 5 additional each week until she is capable of doing 20 to 30 incline legs lifts at which point she should be ready for tuck leg lifts on a bar.

Exercise: Tuck leg lifts with Negative Lower Down

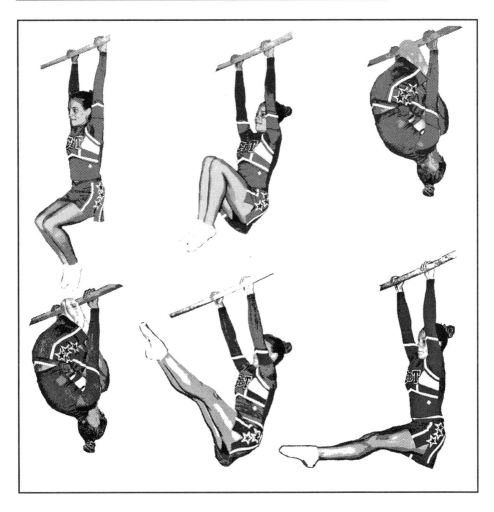

Purpose: To work the full range of motion of the abdominal and hip flexors to build strength and stability in the mid-section of the body.

Set Up: This exercise may be performed on a stall bar, a high bar, or the upper rail (bar) on a set of uneven bars. Note: On any free-standing bar you may want to put a spotting block behind the athlete to stop her legs at the bottom and keep her from developing a swing during subsequent repetitions.

Directions: From a long hang position with an overgrip, the athlete tucks her knees up to her chest and continues to roll her body upward and backward until she can touch her toes to the high bar while her heels are still in contact with the back of her thighs. From this position, the athlete begins to slowly unroll keeping her toes at the bar until her legs have fully straightened. At this point, she slowly lowers her "straight" legs down to a pike position which she holds for three seconds before lowering all the way and beginning the next repetition.

Duration: 3 to 6 lifts, or as many as possible by herself, and then continue rolling as high as possible before lowering to a pike hold.

Note: As with other abdominal exercises the ideal is to maintain tension on the muscles throughout the set of repetitions. On leg lifts, the athlete lowers to a hollow position at the bottom of the repetition. Allowing an arch or a swing could lead to the athlete using a kipping action to help snap her legs up into the next repetition. Any break in form or alteration of the exercise is not acceptable and could lead to an unexpected loss of grip and potential injury.

Exercise: Beyond Handstands

Purpose: To build strength in the lower abdominals and hip flexors and to train the athlete in controlling her body in the inverted position.

Set Up: Use a section of the floor exercise carpet next to a wall or place an open panel on the floor next to a wall.

Directions: The athlete places her hands on the floor in front of the wall a distance roughly equal to the length of her lower leg and kicks up and through a handstand to finish in an arched, inverted position with her feet against the wall. For this position, the athlete pulls primarily through her abdominals and hip flexors to recover her body to a hollow handstand position. The arms and shoulders will participate in this movement by pushing out and back but the gymnast should not kick her legs or push off the wall with her feet to aid in the accomplishment of any repetition.

Duration: 3 to 6 repetitions. This is an auxiliary exercise mostly designed for awareness training not strength development.

Safety: It is very important that you instruct the athlete to breathe normally throughout this exercise. Some athletes have a tendency to hold their breath and strain, which can put excess pressure on small capillaries in the face, eyes, ears, and other structures causing them to rupture and may lead to serious injury.

Back & Side Exercises

Unfortunately, many athletes focus most of their energies disproportionately on abdominal exercises and neglect to strengthen the muscles on their backs or sides.

A common injury, the rhomboid strain occurs when the chest muscles are quickly and forcefully contracted. The rhomboids act like a brake on a car to slow down the speed of motion toward the end of the movement. If the much larger chest muscles overpower the smaller and in many cases weaker rhomboid muscles, a muscle strain could occur.

The key, as with all parts of the body, is to work both the flexor and extensor muscle groups so there is no deficiency in either group.

Exercise: Under Bar Rowing

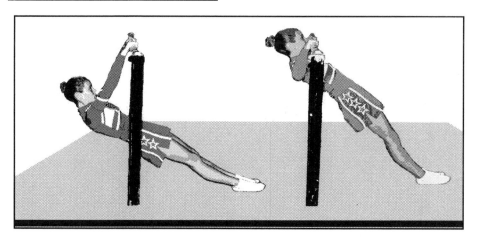

Purpose: To help strengthen upper back muscles (rhomboids).

Set Up: The easiest place to perform this exercise is on a low bar of the uneven bars or a single rail set up.

Directions: The athlete grabs hold of the low bar with an overgrip hand position with her arms shoulder-width apart. From her head to her toes her torso should be perfectly straight with her hips situated almost directly under the bar. From this position, the

61

athlete will pull her chest to the bar keeping her elbows up and in line with her shoulders, and then lower slowly back to the start position.

Duration: Start with 2 sets of 15 seconds each, and then each week as appropriate add 15 seconds to each set (I.E. 30, 45, 60)

Note: You can also increase resistance on this exercise by having the gymnast place her feet up on a small block or stacked panel mats.

Exercise: Lat Pull-ups

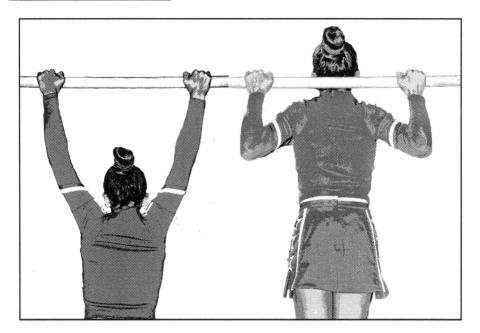

Purpose: To help develop the latissimus dorsi muscle, a prime mover in adduction of the arms (bringing the arms down and closer to the body).

Set Up: This skill should be practiced on a low bar, positioned by setting the bar low or by adding mats, so the athlete can literally stand up with her shoulders touching the bar.

Directions: *(For safety's sake have the athlete start this drill on a low bar where she must bend her knees to keep from touching the floor.)* The athlete places her hands on the low bar in an overgrip about six inches wider than she would for a normal pull-up. By hanging under the bar with her knees bent so the top of her feet and toes touch the floor, the athlete will pull-up, ducking her head slightly forward so the finish position at the top has the bar lightly touching her shoulders. If necessary, she can use her toes to push off the floor slightly during the learning phase of this skill.

Duration: 2 to 4 lat pulls to start, then add 1 lat pull every other week, or 2 negative lat pulls, until the athlete can complete 6 to 10 repetitions.

Negative Lat Pulls: It is quite likely that the athlete will be unable to do more than one or two lat pulls at the start, if any. If this is the case have her start in a standing position with her shoulders at the bar and her hands in overgrip about six inches wider than her shoulders. From this position she can pull down on the bar to hold at shoulder height while lifting her feet off the ground and slowly lowering into a hang position with bent knees under the bar. Have her practice this way until she can do a positive lat pull on her own.

Safety: As stated in other bar exercises, the pull-up action should be smooth and clean, no kipping, jerking, or bouncing. *It is especially important that you make the athlete understand proper technique and that a lack of attention on her part toward the end of the pull-up could cause her to strike the back of her head or neck on the bar, which could lead to potential injury. Never allow the athlete to lean her head back and "rest" on the bar at the peak of this exercise.*

<u>Special Safety Note:</u> **For all chin-up, pull-up, and lat pull-up style exercises, it may be safest to start the athlete on a bar that is low enough that she can put her feet on the floor in case she loses her grip on the bar.**

It is quite common for the muscles in the forearm and hand to tire faster than the muscles of the upper arm and shoulder. As a result, the athlete's forearm begins to numb and she may complain of not being able to maintain her grip as the smaller muscles tire and lose their ability to function, which could cause the athlete to lose her grip and fall from the bar at an inopportune moment.

Exercise: Arch Ups - Floor

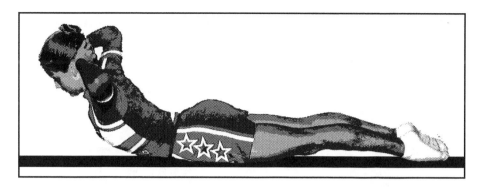

Purpose: To help develop the erector spinae muscle group, a muscle group that helps the athlete to snap up her upper body quickly when snapping down from a back handspring and leading into another handspring or setting for a somersault.

Set Up: This exercise can be performed on the floor exercise with a partner holding that athlete's feet, or by placing her feet under some landing cushions to stabilize her lower body.

Directions: Starting in a prone position on the floor, the athlete places the fingertips of each hand behind her ears or just touching together on the back of her head – do not lock fingers together. Then, the athlete carefully lifts her head and shoulders off the floor as high as possible and momentarily pauses at the peak of motion before slowly lowering back to the floor.

Note: As with abdominal exercises, the idea during the set is to lower to a point where there is still tension on the upper back muscles, and then begin the next repetition – do not allow the athlete to relax on the floor between repetitions.

Duration: Start with 2 sets of 15 seconds each and add 15 seconds each week as proficiency and strength increase until the athlete is able to do sets of 60 seconds each.

Exercise: Arch Ups from a Block

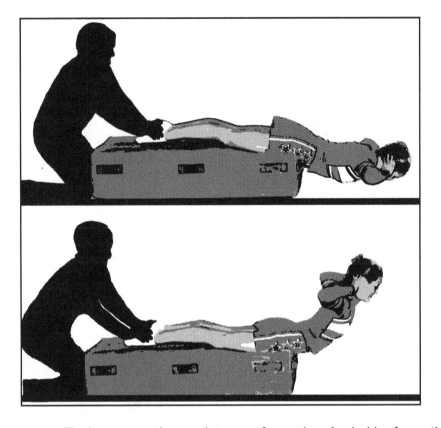

Purpose: To increase the resistance from the Arch Up from the floor. This may also be done with a twist.

Set Up: Use the top section of a trapezoid, a small spotting block or a couple of folded and stacked panel mats. The athlete will need a partner to hold her legs securely.

Directions: The same as the above directions with the exception that the athlete is situated on a spotting block or stack of folded panel mats so her hip to her feet are on the mat and being held in place by a partner.

Duration: Start with 2 sets of 15 seconds each and add 15 seconds each week as proficiency and strength increase until the athlete is able to do sets of 60 seconds each.

Safety: Make sure the person holding the athlete's legs warns the athlete when she is going to release her legs so the athlete does not crash face first into the floor.

Exercise: Arch Up with Torso Twist

Purpose: To work oblique aspects of the erector spinae group and to possibly include serratus anterior muscles.

Set Up: This exercise can be performed on the floor exercise with a partner holding the athlete's feet, or by placing her feet under some landing cushions to stabilize her lower body.

Directions: Virtually the same as "Arch Ups" from the floor, except as the athlete nears the peak of motion she will twist her torso alternately to the right or left on each repetition.

Duration: Start with 2 sets of 15 seconds each and add 15 seconds each week as proficiency and strength increase until the athlete is able to do sets of 60 seconds each.

Exercise: Side Arches

Purpose: To build strength in the oblique muscles, serratus anterior, intercostals, and quadratus lumborum, basically all the muscles used to pull the body into a side arch position, which help with the twisting skills.

Set Up: The easiest place to practice this exercise is on a floor exercise carpet right up next to a wall or against a stable and secure spotting block.

Directions: Starting in a prone position next to a wall or a secure and stable spotting block, the athlete executes a ¼ turn so she is on her side with her back to the wall or block, and she has both arms raised above her head. From this position, the athlete lifts upper body and legs simultaneously as high as possible and holds at the peak of motion for one second before lowering carefully back to the ground. Once proficient, the athlete can add a folded panel mat, which only her hips rest on to add a wider range of motion.

Duration: Start with 2 sets of 15 seconds each and add 15 seconds each week as proficiency and strength increase until the athlete is able to do sets of 60 seconds each.

Exercise: Side Sit Ups

Purpose: To build strength in the oblique muscles, serratus anterior, intercostals, and quadratus lumborum, basically all the muscles used to pull the body into a side arch position, which help with the twisting skills.

Set Up: Use the top section of a trapezoid, a small spotting block or a couple of folded and stacked panel mats. The athlete will need a partner to hold her legs securely.

Directions: Starting on her side with her knees bent and secured by a partner, the athlete positions her hips just at the edge of the block so her upper body is suspended and parallel to the floor exercise carpet. With the fingers of both hands touching the sides or back of her head, the athlete sits up sideways, pauses for one second at the peak of motion and then lowers until her upper body is parallel to the floor, and then starts her next repetition.

Duration: Start with 2 sets of 15 seconds each and add 15 seconds each week as proficiency and strength increase until the athlete is able to do sets of 60 seconds each.

Planning the Work; Working the Plan

Everyone here, coaches and athletes, should have had a chance to peruse the book by now, so you should have a good idea of some of the exercises available. All that is left now is developing a plan that is specific to the needs of your program and always specific to the needs of the individual athlete.

Unfortunately, any strength circuit, no matter how well thought out is a one-size fits all proposition. There are just too many variables to take into account. A "strength-building" plan must take into account the needs of the individual, if for no other reason, than for safety's sake.

The following pages contain a series of charts:

- A strength and flexibility testing / evaluation.
- A sample "strength circuit plan / suggested guidelines" for a five week period.
- A blank copy of a strength circuit plan so you can develop an individual or a group workout plan.

Goal #1 (after medical evaluations)

Evaluate the strength and flexibility of every squad member and record the results. Use the results obtained as a base score for each athlete to determine her progress in subsequent tests.

What skills do you test? That may change based on the focus of your program throughout the season, so the form is blank allowing you to choose which elements to test. You may choose to start with some basic elements like: Leg Lifts, Pull-ups, Parallel Bar Dips, Vertical Height Jump, Splits (right & left), Middle Split, Bridge, and Shoulder Flexibility.[8]

---

[8] These are some of the classic elements tested in the women's JEDP gymnastics program.

71

Goal #2

Based on the results of the above test, develop a strength circuit that meets the needs of the largest number of squad members to make the most effective use of workout time. You do not need to use every single exercise listed in this book! In fact, due to time constraints you may need to develop a circuit that contains only 8 – 12 or at the most 12 – 14 exercises. Use your best judgment or call a local college / university Physical Education department for guidelines and suggestions.

Safety Note: Even with this plan, you may still need to set up side stations in your circuit plan to help athletes overcome specific weaknesses or to work modified circuits. No one plan will fit every athlete. There will always be those who can do more than the suggested number of sets and repetitions and those that do less. The key is that everybody does the best they are capable of at the moment.

Special Note: Whenever partnering athletes together, make sure they are of similar size and are capable of spotting safely and effectively or you (the coach) may have to supervise and spot that particular circuit station.

Goal #3

Test strength and flexibility every four to six weeks and record the results. Increase the resistance by modifying the exercise to use more of the athlete's weight during each repetition.

Goal #4

Develop a maintenance plan. After three or four testings, you may notice that your squad members are leveling out on their test scores. At this point you may want to develop a maintenance level strength circuit that is less time consuming but still hits the major muscles of the body, especially the core stabilizing muscles.

Goal #5

Switch to more sport specific exercises. Once your athletes attain the basic level of strength necessary, you may choose to switch to sport specific exercises like multiple series of round off back handsprings, multiple split leaps and jumps on the trampoline or tumble tramp, etc. Performing the actual skill as an exercise helps develop the peripheral muscles used in the specific sequence and timing appropriate to the skill.

(Athlete's Names)

Strength / Flexibility Tracking Date: _____									
Strength Skills									
Flexibility Skills									

| Day of the Week | SAMPLE STRENGTH CIRCUIT | Sets & Reps / Weeks 1 – 5 of each Month |

M	T	W	R	F	S	Name of Exercise	S	R	S	R	S	R	S	R	S	R
	X					Block Pushes	2	4	1	8	2	5	1	10	1	10
X				X		Mushies (15 sec. sets)	2	?	1	30 sec	2	20 sec	1	45 sec	1	45 sec
X				X		Reverse Leg Lift (floor) (each leg)	2	6	2	8	2	10	1	15	1	15
	X					Hamstring Push Ups	2	4	2	6	1	8	1	8	1	10
X				X		Side Lunges (passes on floor)	2	4	2	4	1	6	1	6	1	8
	X					Spiders (passes on floor)	2	4	2	4	2	6	1	8	1	8
X	X			X		Heel Raises (each leg)	2	6	2	6	2	8	2	8	2	10
X	X			X		Under Bar Pull Ups (Rowing)	2	4	2	4	2	5	2	5	2	6
X				X		Pull Ups (or Negatives)	1	4	2	3	2	3	2	4	2	4
	X					Lat Pull Ups (low bar)	2	4	2	4	2	5	2	5	2	6
X				X		Bent Knee Push Ups	2	4	2	4	2	6	2	6	2	8
	X					Triceps Push Ups	2	4	2	4	2	5	2	5	2	6
X	X			X		Chin Ups – Low Bar	2	4	2	4	2	5	2	5	2	6
X	X			X		½ Tuck Sit Ups	2	8	2	10	2	12	2	30 sec	2	30 sec
X	X			X		Tucked Leg Lifts	2	4	2	4	2	6	2	6	2	8
X	X			X		Side Arches	2	4	2	4	2	6	2	6	2	8
X	X			X		Upper Crunches (hold 2 sec.)	2	8	2	10	2	10	1	12	1	12
X	X			X		Lower Crunches (hold 2 sec.)	2	8	2	10	2	10	1	12	1	12
X	X			X		Arch Ups	2	6	2	6	1	8	1	8	1	10

Day of the Week   **Sets & Reps / Weeks 1 – 4 of each Month**

M	T	W	R	F	S	Name of Exercise	S	R	S	R	S	R	S	R	S	R

See "Free Articles" at **www.GymnasticsTrainingTips.com** for blank 8.5" X 11" forms.

Body Position Chart

Tuck   Squat   Pike

Closed Pike   Straddle   Closed Straddle

Pike Stand   Forward Split   Bridge / Back Bend

Straddle Stand   Lunge   Stretch Position

Layout   Prone

Flexibility

The main focus of this book is on strength, however, I would be remiss if I did not include at least a smattering of information about warming up before, cooling down after, and the importance of flexibility.

Importance of flexibility

Flexibility can be defined as the ability to move a body part or parts through the broadest range of motion possible, while maintaining strength and stability in the respective joint.

Flexibility is one of the showcase abilities of most accomplished cheerleaders. In fact, most pictures displayed in print and online media depict a cheerleader exhibiting some unusual / extraordinary form of flexibility. Unusual, that is for the rest of us mere mortals. Yet flexibility is one of the key ingredients for success in any level of cheerleading endeavor (not to mention several other sports as well).

Several cheerleading skills contain elements of dance and leaps that dynamically lengthen the muscles in the legs. Other skills like the back walkover demonstrate shoulder and back flexibility in a graceful but more subdued manner. Regardless of the quality of movement, explosive or subdued, the ability to safely extend  the muscles, tendons, and ligaments through the necessary range of motion is crucial in the prevention of injury. Muscles, tendons, and ligaments that are tight through lack of flexibility or improper warm-up are an injury waiting to happen.

Many people consider cheerleaders to be naturally limber and flexible, but in several cases that is just not true. An easy test of your flexibility[9] is to sit on the floor with your legs together, the back of your knees touching the floor, with your toes pointing toward the ceiling. Slowly reach forward, past your ankles if you can, without straining or bouncing the upper body. The average child can barely reach one half of an inch past her ankles.

You may be more or less flexible than the example above[10], however, as a cheerleader performing dynamic and explosive leaps and jumps you do want to make sure you are sufficiently flexible to prevent injury.

The basics of flexibility are:

1. **The Warm Up: Get the blood flowing first.** Have the athlete run a few laps around the floor exercise carpet or do some jumping jacks to get the blood flowing out to the extremities. Microscopic muscle tears may occur when you stretch a "cold" muscle. (See suggested "Warm Up & Aerobic Activity" circuit on page 60)

   At the beginning of the workout you may perform basic stretches designed by your coach to prepare your muscles for activity, although some recent articles suggest that stretching for flexibility should occur after the workout and possibly after any strength training sessions for maximum effectiveness[11].

---

[9] Note this is a general test for hamstring flexibility; this gives no indication of flexibility in other joints of the body. Flexibility is specific to the joint tested and may not be the same for a similar but opposite body part (I.E. right shoulder can be more flexible than left shoulder).

[10] Athlete should be showing a straighter back position with feet flexed more as per the text.

[11] "Recently however, data has been presented from studies on adults which have shown that static stretching immediately prior to performing powerful activities reduces performance (for example, Kokkonen, Nelson, " Cornwell, 1998; Nelson, Cornwell, " Heise, 1996)." [Mcneal, J. R. Ph.D. and Wm. A. Sands, Ph.D. Static Stretching Reduces Power Production in Gymnasts. Technique magazine. © 2001 USA Gymnastics, Indianapolis.] www.usa-gymnastics.org/publications/technique/2001/10/stretching.html .

2. **Perform the stretch in a controlled manner.** For our purpose here I will briefly describe only two types of stretching: **ballistic and static.**

Ballistic is a type of stretch where the body is in motion, usually some form of bouncing. Any type of bouncing or flopping into a stretch position can cause tears in the muscle tissue and put undue strain on tendons and ligaments. In addition, the body has what is known as the *stretch reflex*. When you step off a curb and start to twist your ankle, your body uses the stretch reflex to snatch your ankle back before it can be injured. If, through excess force, you overpower this reflex you can tear muscle tissue, strain tendons, or sprain your ankle. You may even cause what is known as an avulsion fracture where the tendon pulls off a piece of bone. In cheerleading, **ballistic stretching may not be ideal**.

Static stretching occurs when you extend a body part to the end of its normal range of motion and then carefully extend that range until you begin to feel mild discomfort. Then, hold that position for thirty seconds to a minute. For the general cheerleading population, this may be the most appropriate form of stretching.

3. Continue to **breathe evenly** and relax while stretching. Allow yourself to slowly **sink into the stretch** as you relax the tension in the muscle.
4. Work with your coach to **develop** a **specific** set of stretching **exercises** for an overall body stretch and specific exercises for problem areas such as splits or shoulder stretches, etc.

5. **Isolate** the area you are stretching. Most young athletes tend to take the path of least resistance. Unfortunately, that can mean potential injury. Make sure you keep your body alignment appropriate to the stretch being performed, and isolate and stretch only the specific muscle group according to the respective stretch. Failure to do so could cause you to stretch the wrong body parts and open yourself to the possibility of injury.

6. **Vary** the stretching routine every few months to keep boredom and sloppy performance from becoming normal behavior.

Warm Up & Aerobic Activity

Start by rolling out your ankles and wrists, maybe doing a few jumping jacks, then start the following drills following the perimeter of the floor exercise mat.

1. Sprinting / Jogging **2 X around the mat**
2. Chassés
       A. Facing inside **Once each direction**
       B. Facing outside **Once each direction**

Walk two laps around the mat.

3. Skipping **2 X around the mat**
4. Split Leaps **10 on each leg**

Walk two laps around the mat.

Stationary Aerobic Drills

1. Big Hops / Little Hops (on both feet) **10 each.**
2. Hops: Right foot only, Left foot only **10 each.**
3. Hopping both feet side to side **10 each**
4. Hopping front and back **10 each**
5. Full turn jumps **5 to each side.**

Coordination Drills
Right leg split leap, left leg split leap, straddle jump, jumping jack, jump full turn, tuck jump (start over from the beginning).
5 times in place

Walk two laps to lower, heart rate.

This "Warm-Up & Aerobic Activity" circuit should take at least 10 minutes if done correctly!

Cool Down

When ending any dynamic or vigorous activity it may not be the best idea to just plop down on the mat and start stretching. The sudden ending of a dynamic activity could cause your blood to flow to your extremities and make you feel faint.

If your strength circuit or workout activities leave you breathless or with an elevated heart rate, it may be best to walk a few laps around the floor exercise carpet allowing your heart rate to return to normal before stretching for flexibility. While walking you can roll out your wrists, neck, and shoulders.

Basic Stretches for Flexibility

Splits (right & left) (30 – 60 seconds each)

Seated Straddle (Closed position stretching for 30–60 seconds each to the right leg, left leg, and finally chest to the ground in the center.)

Seated Pike (Closed position stretching bring the chest to the knees with a flat back and tight knees.)

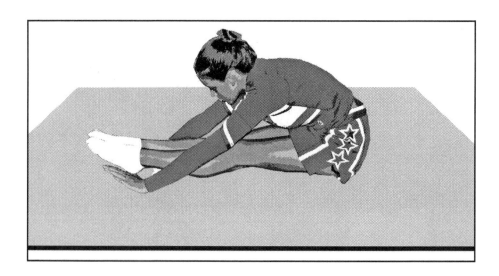

Bridge

Calf Stretch

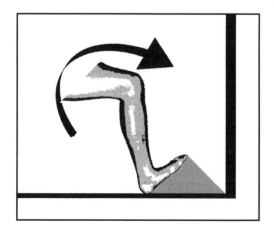

Shoulder Stretch

Quad / Hamstring Stretch

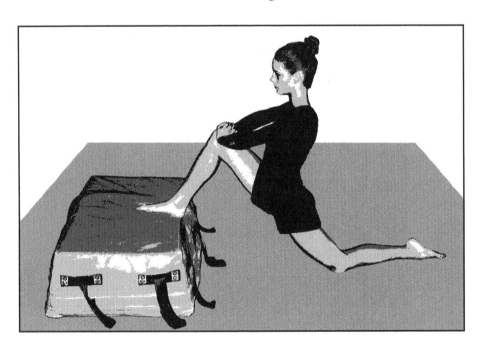

For more information on flexibility and appropriate stretching exercises, please see your coach.

Commercial Interlude

The stretches listed above are the most basic included in most flexibility circuits. The focus of this book is on strength, however, so you will be overjoyed, breathless with anticipation and fidgety like a child waiting for Christmas morning when you realize another book is coming soon with the focus on (Ta Da!) *"Flexibility."*

And, don't forget to check out the highly acclaimed "Back Handsprings: The Secret Techniques," also available at: www.GymnasticsTrainingTips.com .

Home Workouts

It is possible to get some safety equipment like mats and purchase a chin-up bar from a sporting goods store and develop a workout area at home. But, it is still suggested-demanded-required that you have appropriate supervision by an adult during this time.

- All exercise should be performed in a clear and safe workout area.

Carolina Gym Supply
1-877-496-7883

- Practice only the exercises approved by your coach.

- Do not adapt technique without guidance from your coach.

- Check the stability of any equipment you use in your home circuit, such as a chin-up bar in the doorway – make sure it is adjusted and secured and is appropriate for your weight and activity. A qualified adult / carpenter should make sure the device is properly secured.

- Invest in tumbling mats to workout on and use them in your exercise program.

- You may want to invest in surgical tubing or Thera-bands[12] to practice some sport-specific motions at home with some resistance. Consult with your coach first.

Supervision

Since most athletes tend to take the path of least resistance when tired, the supervising adult can make sure you follow the path to true enlightenment and strength development. Besides getting parents involved in doing the strength circuit with the athlete, along with eating at Subway like Jared, could make for a happy and healthy family.

---

[12] http://www.thera-band.com/home_fitness.html

Glossary of Terms

Abduction – 1) In a perfect world what would happen to your adoring adolescent between the ages of 13 and 21, or 2) a movement of a body part or parts away from the midline (think spine) of the body. Lifting your right leg laterally and upward is abduction of the right leg.

Adduction is the opposite of abduction because you "add" or bring a body part closer to the midline of your body. As in the example above, lowering your right leg and bringing it together with the left leg is adduction.

Body composition normally relates to what percentage of your body weight is made of lean tissue and muscle, and what percentage of your body weight is made up of fat. Your optimum body composition should be determined by evaluation from a qualified medical practitioner.

Cardiovascular relates to the heart and respiratory system. Cardiovascular activities are those normally associated with endurance type activities.

Circuit. A series of exercises designed to be performed in a specific order and sometimes within a specific time frame.

Concentric is an action that causes a muscle to shorten.

Eccentric motion, or forced lengthening, occurs when a force or resistance causes a shortened or flexed muscle to extend while still attempting to contract. Slowly lowering from a pull-up is an example of eccentric motion.

Extend or extension is most easily illustrated when a leg is bent and then straightened or extended.

Flex or flexion is most commonly associated with bending the arm to demonstrate a large upper arm muscle (the biceps). When will girls stop showing off their guns?

Flexibility. 1) A state of mind required by all parents and coaches of adolescent athletes, or 2) flexibility can be described as the range of motion a body part has with relation to another body part or possibly an outside apparatus.

Frequency. 1) The coordinates on your child's iPOD or radio for obnoxious music, if you can call it music, or 2) how often a particular exercise or series of exercises is performed.

Intensity describes the degree of effort applied to an activity.

Isometric is contraction of muscle tissue that causes no motion.

Ligament is a connective tissue in the body from bone to bone.

Maintenance is a system of exercise that sustains a specific conditioning level but is not usually as time consuming or intense as the effort needed to get to that level in the first place.

Muscle. Contractile (shortens) tissue that causes flexion, extension, or stabilization of a body part or parts.

Negative. 1) An adolescent with a bad attitude, or 2) the eccentric lengthening of a muscle as when the athlete lowers from a pull-up back to the start position.

Positive. 1) Someone who is a pleasure to be around, or 2) the act of shortening a muscle or muscles to complete the first half of any exercise repetition.

Recovery. 1) A rehabilitation center where most parents and coaches end up after years of working with adolescent young women, or 2) the resting time between sets of exercises or 3) the resting and recuperating time needed between workouts.

Reps or Repetitions. The number of times a particular exercise or skill is performed in one set.

Resistance. 1) The typical response from any adolescent when you request her help or you are providing guidance, or 2) an amount of force a muscle or group of muscles must overcome to produce a desired movement or exercise.

Set. A series of repetitions of one exercise or drill. For example, 5 push-ups may equal one set. Two sets would be 5 push-upss, a brief recovery period or rest, then the next set of 5 push-ups.

Strength. 1) What coaches and parents pray for most of the time; or 2) the level of force muscular tissue can provide in a particular movement or series of movements.

Tendon is a connective tissue from muscle to bone.

About the Author

Several pizzas and many years ago, Rik Feeney was a competitive gymnast through High School and Temple University. During his career, Rik owned and worked at private gymnastics clubs where he trained gymnasts from state to national level competitors.

Rik is the author of several books on the sport of gymnastics, the first of which was *"Gymnastics: A Guide for Parents and Athletes"* – available via email at **www.GymnasticsTrainingTips.com**.

He has gone on to ghostwrite and continue authoring books with a new series titled "Gymnastics Education Modules" or **GEM's** ™ which include techniques for popular gymnastics and tumbling skills as well as information for parents and spectators.

If you have any new ideas for techniques you would like to add to this document or have comments for the author, you can send them care of **coachrik@aol.com** .

Richardson Publishing is looking for material from new authors. If you have an idea or specialized knowledge you believe would make a good book or booklet, send a query letter care of the address listed on the back cover or publication page of this book.

www.GymnasticsTrainingTips.com

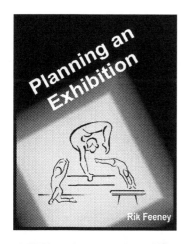

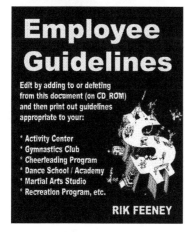

www.GymnasticsTrainingTips.com

CPSIA information can be obtained
at www.ICGtesting.com
Printed in the USA
BVHW072242141218
535685BV00008B/461/P